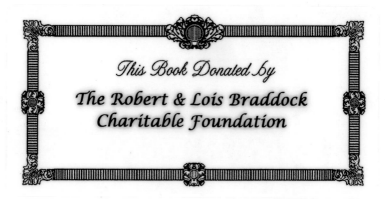

AMERICAN HEROES

PHILLIS WHEATLEY

She Loved Words

Boston's Old South Meeting House

AMERICAN HEROES

PHILLIS WHEATLEY

She Loved Words

SNEED B. COLLARD III

Marshall Cavendish
Benchmark
New York

For Laura and Emile

Marshall Cavendish Benchmark
99 White Plains Road
Tarrytown, New York 10591
www.marshallcavendish.us

Library of Congress Cataloging-in-Publication Data
Collard, Sneed B.
Phillis Wheatley: she loved words / by Sneed B. Collard III.
p. cm. — (American heroes)
Summary: "A juvenile biography of Phillis Wheatley, America's first black poet"—Provided by publisher.
Includes bibliographical references and index.
ISBN 978-0-7614-4057-4
1. Wheatley, Phillis, 1753-1784—Juvenile literature. 2. Poets, American—Colonial period,
ca. 1600-1775—Biography—Juvenile literature. 3. African American poets—Biography—Juvenile literature.
4. Slaves—United States—Biography—Juvenile literature. I. Title.
PS866.W5Z5829 2009
811'.1—dc22
[B]
2008044947

Editor: Joyce Stanton
Publisher: Michelle Bisson
Art Director: Anahid Hamparian
Series Designer: Anne Scatto
Printed in Malaysia
1 3 5 6 4 2

Images provided by Debbie Needleman, Picture Researcher, Portsmouth, NH, from the following sources: *Front Cover:* Archives and Special Collections Department, Healey Library, University of Massachusetts at Boston. *Back Cover:* View of Boston Common. C. 1750 (wool, silk, metallic threads and beads on linen ground) by Hannah Otis (1732-1801) ©Museum of Fine Arts, Boston, Massachusetts, USA/The Bridgeman Art Library. *Pages i, 34:* Archives and Special Collections Department, Healey Library, University of Massachusetts at Boston; *pages ii, 7, 12:* North Wind Picture Archives; *page vi:* Old State House, Boston, 1801 (oil on panel) by James Brown Marston (1775-1817). ©Massachusetts Historical Society/The Bridgeman Art Library; *page 1:* Courtesy of the Massachusetts Historical Society; *page 3:* Ann Ronan Picture Library/HIP/Art Resource, NY; *pages 4, 8, 11:* The Granger Collection, New York; *page 15:* Shipwreck off a Rocky Coast (oil on canvas) by Thomas Buttersworth (1768-1842) Yale Center for British Art. Paul Mellon Collection, USA/The Bridgeman Art Library; *page 16:* John Collet/Private Collection/The Bridgeman Art Library/Getty Images; *page 19:* National Portrait Gallery, Smithsonian Institution, Art Resource, NY; *page 20:* Photograph ©2009 Museum of Fine Arts, Boston; *page 23:* Stock Montage/Getty Images; *page 24:* Title page and frontispiece to "Poems on Various Subjects, Religious and Moral" by Phillis Wheatley (1753-84) published in London, 1773 (engraving) by English School. ©Massachusetts Historical Society. Boston, MA./The Bridgeman Art Library; *page 27:* Balthasar Nebot/The Bridgeman Art Library/Getty Images; *page 29:* Samuel King/The Bridgeman Art Library/Getty Images; *page 31:* ©Nancy Carter/North Wind Picture Archives; *page 32:* ©Jeff Greenberg/Alamy

CONTENTS

Phillis lived in Boston, Massachusetts, in the 1700s,
when America was still ruled by Great Britain.

Phillis Wheatley

In the fall of 1772, Phillis Wheatley sat before eighteen of Boston's leading men. The men had one purpose: to find out if a slave girl really could write poetry. One by one, the men began asking Phillis questions—hard questions about poetry, religion, and other subjects. Phillis answered their questions thoughtfully and intelligently. The men decided that, yes, this slave girl really was a poet. The experience revealed a lot about Phillis Wheatley.

It revealed even more about America.

Phillis Wheatley was not born a slave. She was born a free person in West Africa. In 1761, when she was about seven years old, she was captured by slave traders and put on a ship to America. The journey was a horrible one. Captains of slave ships crammed their human cargo into tiny spaces. The slaves were fed small meals of awful food. They did not have enough clothing and were rarely allowed exercise. Many children, women, and men died on these voyages. Phillis arrived in Boston weak and sick.

Phillis was born a free person. She was captured
by slave traders when she was a young girl.

NEGROES,
TO BE SOLD

A Parcel of young able bodied Negro Men, one of whom is a Cooper by Trade, two Negroes Wenches, and likewise two Girls, one of 12 Years old, and the other 16, the latter a good Seemſtreſs, and can be well recommended.

In America, Phillis was put up for sale as a slave.

In Boston, Phillis was put up for sale at a slave auction. At this time, it was still legal to buy and sell human beings in all thirteen of the American colonies. The slave traders probably didn't think anyone would buy Phillis. She did not look strong or healthy enough to do much work. She might even die soon. Who would want to spend money on such a girl?

Phillis, though, caught the eye of a woman named Susanna Wheatley. Susanna needed a companion, and her heart reached out to the young captive. Susanna and her husband, John, bought the sickly girl for a small amount of money. They took her home. They named her Phillis after the slave ship that had brought her to America.

*Her new masters named Phillis after the slave ship
that brought her to America.*

Phillis was treated kindly in the Wheatleys' home, almost as one of the family.

The Wheatleys treated Phillis almost as one of the family. She ate at their dinner table. She was kept separate from the other slaves. Even so, she suffered from asthma and other health problems. Because of this, the Wheatleys gave her only light chores to do around the house. Soon, though, Phillis began to surprise her masters.

Not long after joining the Wheatleys' household, Phillis began showing an interest in reading and writing. She watched the Wheatleys read books, and began using charcoal and chalk to copy letters of the alphabet. Seeing this interest, Susanna Wheatley asked her daughter, Mary, to teach Phillis to read and write. Within two years, Phillis mastered the English language. She began studying Latin, history, mythology, and the sciences.

Soon, Phillis showed a passion for language and learning.

Phillis had a special love for religion and poetry.

Under Susanna's influence, Phillis took a special interest in the Bible. She studied the Bible for many hours. She talked about it with the rest of the Wheatley family. Phillis also began going to church with the Wheatleys. In 1771, when she was seventeen years old, Phillis was baptized and became a Christian herself.

All of this time, Phillis nurtured a love for poetry. She felt a special connection with the poet Alexander Pope. Pope wrote about society and human nature. His words helped inspire Phillis to write her own poetry.

Even in her early poems, Phillis showed her passion for God and religion. When she was about thirteen years old, she wrote a poem about two men, Hussey and Coffin, who survived a famous shipwreck. In her poem, she asks: if the men had died, would their souls have gone to heaven or to hell?

Suppose the groundless Gulph [Gulf] had snatch'd away
Hussey and Coffin to the raging Sea;
Where wou'd they go? where wou'd be their Abode?
With the supreme and independent God,
Or made their Beds down in the Shades below . . .

In 1767, Susanna Wheatley sent this poem to a Rhode Island newspaper. It became the first poem Phillis ever had published.

The first poem Phillis had published, in 1767, was about a famous shipwreck.

Phillis's poem about the Reverend George Whitefield
attracted attention on both sides of the Atlantic.

Phillis also began writing elegies [EL-e-jeez]. An elegy is a poem of sorrow for someone who is dead. Phillis wrote one elegy for a famous preacher named George Whitefield. The poem was published all over the American colonies and even in Great Britain. After this success, Susanna Wheatley decided to try to get an entire book of Phillis's poems published.

There was one problem: many people did not believe a slave girl could really write poetry herself.

In the 1700s, most people did not think that people with dark skin were equal to people with lighter skin. Thomas Jefferson wrote that all men were created equal, but even he did not think that black people were as intelligent as white people. When Susanna Wheatley tried to get Phillis's poems put into a book, publishers refused. They simply didn't believe that a slave girl could write such fine poems.

Thomas Jefferson wrote the Declaration of Independence. He declared that all men were created equal. But where did that leave the black people?

John Hancock and seventeen other leading men
were very impressed with Phillis.

To solve that problem, the Wheatleys arranged for eighteen of Boston's leading men to question Phillis. The group included ministers, poets, and the governor of Massachusetts. It also included John Hancock, who would later sign the Declaration of Independence. The men were very impressed with Phillis. They signed a letter saying that Phillis really had written her poetry. American publishers still refused to publish Phillis's book. With the letter, however, Susanna was able to get the poems published in Britain.

Poems on Various Subjects, Religious and Moral was published in 1773. It included elegies. It included poems about God and religion. It included thoughts about nature. But Phillis had also watched the American Revolution taking shape. Just down the street from the Wheatley house, Americans had protested against unfair taxes that the British king had forced on them. It is not surprising that Phillis also wrote about this subject—and about freedom—in her poems.

America's struggle for freedom shaped some of Phillis's poems.

Published according to Act of Parliament, Sept.ʳ 1, 1773 by Arch.ᵈ Bell,
Bookseller Nº 8 near the Saracens Head Aldgate.

POEMS

ON

VARIOUS SUBJECTS,

RELIGIOUS AND MORAL.

BY

PHILLIS WHEATLEY,

NEGRO SERVANT TO MR. JOHN WHEATLEY,
of BOSTON, in NEW ENGLAND.

L O N D O N:
Printed for A. BELL, Bookseller, Aldgate; and sold by
Meſſrs. COX and BERRY, King-Street, *BOSTON.*
M DCC LXXIII.

Poems on Various Subjects, Religious and Moral *proved to many people
that black people could be as intelligent and thoughtful as anyone else.*

Phillis's book made her famous both in Great Britain and America. It was the first poetry book published in English by a person of African descent. Some people did not like Phillis's poems. They thought she was just copying other poets. But for many others, Phillis proved that black people—even slaves—were as intelligent and thoughtful as anyone else.

During the same summer her book was published, Phillis traveled to Britain. She had struggled with her health, and the Wheatleys' doctor thought an ocean voyage might help her. The trip also allowed Phillis to oversee the publication of her book in London. There, she met with many famous people, including Benjamin Franklin. But after only a few weeks in London, she learned that Susanna Wheatley had fallen ill.

Phillis traveled to London to oversee the publication of her book, but her trip was cut short.

Phillis rushed home to take care of Susanna. Unfortunately, Susanna died just a few months later, in 1774. Phillis was devastated. By this time, the Wheatleys had freed Phillis from slavery, but she still felt that they were her family. For the next few years, she continued to live with John Wheatley and his daughter, Mary. Phillis also kept writing. She wrote poems about the American Revolution. She wrote about George Washington, and even paid a visit to the great general himself.

Phillis's poems about George Washington and the American Revolution brought her to the attention of the great general himself.

But hardship lay ahead. First John Wheatley and then Mary died, leaving Phillis homeless. In 1778, she married a free black man, John Peters. Phillis and John had three children. First one baby died, then another. John was unable to pay his bills and so was sent to prison. Phillis tried to get another book of poems published. But during the war years, no one had the interest or money to publish her work. Phillis died on December 5, 1784. Her third—and last—child died a few hours later.

Phillis's life ended in hardship and tragedy.

Today, many schools are named after Phillis in honor of her life and work.

Today, some people think that Phillis did not do enough to speak out against slavery. But Phillis did write about slavery. She did it in her letters and in the hidden language of her poetry. She wanted freedom for both herself and others, but she realized she could not end slavery alone. Like all writers, she worked to share the human experience through her love of words. If she had one wish for her life, it was probably to be remembered as a religious person and a skilled poet—which is how we remember her now.

IMPORTANT DATES

About 1753 or 1754 Born in West Africa, perhaps in Gambia or Senegal.

1761 Brought to Boston aboard the slave ship *Phillis*; purchased by John and Susanna Wheatley.

1765 Writes first poems.

1767 Publishes first poem, "On Messrs Hussey and Coffin."

1770 Publishes "On the Death of the Rev. Mr. George Whitefield, 1770."

1773 Publishes book, *Poems on Various Subjects, Religious and Moral*; travels to London; freed from slavery by the Wheatleys.

1774 Susanna Wheatley dies.

1776 Meets George Washington.

1778 John and Mary Wheatley die; Phillis marries John Peters.

1784 Dies on December 5.

WORDS TO KNOW

African descent Coming from, or having ancestors who came from, Africa.

American Revolution (also called the Revolutionary War or the War for Independence) The war the American colonies fought to win freedom from Great Britain. The Revolution was fought from 1775 to 1781. A peace treaty was officially signed in 1783.

asthma A condition of the lungs that makes breathing difficult.

colonies Places or territories that are ruled by another country. Colonies are often far away from the country that governs them.

Declaration of Independence The famous document that proclaimed that the American colonies were independent from Great Britain.

elegy A poem that expresses sorrow for, or honors, a person who has died.

Latin The language spoken by the ancient Romans; French, Spanish, and Italian are all based on Latin, and English has many words that come from it.

mythology The stories people create to explain the world around them.

publish To print a written work and offer it for sale.

slave A person who is owned by another person.

taxes Fees that governments often charge people on goods they buy, money they earn, or property they own.

TO LEARN MORE ABOUT PHILLIS WHEATLEY

WEB SITES

About.com: Women's History
http://womenshistory.about.com/od/aframerwriters/a/philliswheatley.htm

The Massachusetts Historical Society
http://www.masshist.org/endofslavery/?queryID=57

Memoir of Phillis Wheatley
http://docsouth.unc.edu/neh/thatcher/thatcher.html

Poetry Foundation
http://www.poetryfoundation.org/archive/poet.html?id=81619

BOOKS

Phillis Wheatley: Slave and Poet by Robin S. Doak. Compass Point Books, 2006.

Phillis Wheatley by Susan R. Gregson. Capstone Press, 2000.

Phillis Wheatley: First Published African-American Poet by Deborah Kent. Child's World, 2003.

Phyllis Wheatley: Slave & Poet by Gerald W. Morton.
  PublishAmerica, 2008.

PLACES TO VISIT

The Old South Meeting House
310 Washington Street
Boston, MA 02108
PHONE: (617) 482-6439
WEB SITE: **http://www.oldsouthmeetinghouse.org**

Museum of African American History
46 Joy Street
Boston, MA 02114
PHONE: (617) 720-2991
WEB SITE: **http://www.afroammuseum.org/index.htm**

The Boston Women's Memorial (to see a sculpture of Phillis)
Commonwealth Avenue Mall
Boston, MA
WEB SITE: **http://www.cityofboston.gov/women/memorial.asp**

INDEX

ABOUT THE AUTHOR

SNEED B. COLLARD III is the author of more than fifty award-winning books for young people, including *Science Warriors*; *Wings*; *Pocket Babies*; and the four-book SCIENCE ADVENTURES series for Marshall Cavendish Benchmark. In addition to his writing, Sneed is a popular speaker and presents widely to students, teachers, and the general public. In 2006, he was selected as the Washington Post–Children's Book Guild Nonfiction Award winner for his achievements in children's writing. He is also the author of several novels for young adults, including *Dog Sense*, *Flash Point*, and *Double Eagle*. To learn more about Sneed, visit his Web site at www.sneedbcollardiii.com.